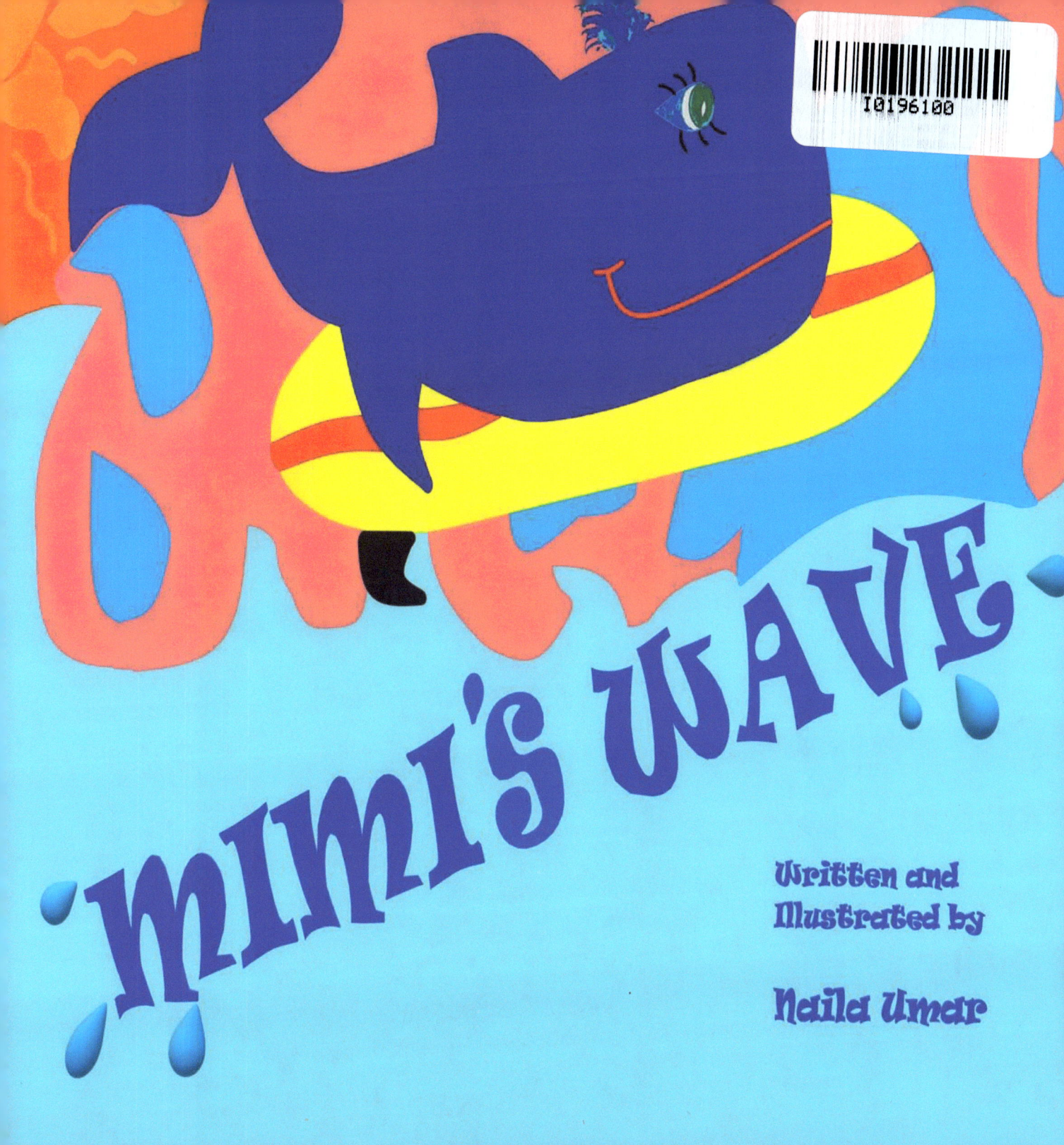

Mimi's Wave

Story made in Canada
KidsBooooksByNaila LLC

Library of Congress 2021

ISBN 978-1-77 5173-1-1

This book is dedicated to all the little groms and gromettes that have a passion for anything! Don't give your passions up. You can do ANYTHING. Also shout out to the love of my life, my grom Xavier, nephews Jaden and Jory and my late brother Javed who always did something rad.

On the west side of the world where the ocean sparkles blue; Lived a whale whose name was Mimi, who was friendly, big and blue!

Now Mimi was a whale who would swim among the waves. Her body moving all around flowing in and out of caves.

She liked to take long swims down near the sandy shore, she liked to watch the waves come crashing down and ROAR!

One day as Mimi took her travels through the misty sea, she saw these people on these boards whose hands were waving free!

They would swim out to the waves that stood so tall and wide; they would wait around so patiently, all searching for the tide.

The waves had started rolling in, the sea was moving past, these people hopped upon their boards and began to paddle fast!

Then suddenly she saw
these people stand up,
their legs so strong.
They all had stood, their
knees were bent, their
boards were short and
long.

What fun she thought, what fun indeed to ride in with the wave. All the time it took to swim and all the time she'd save!

She did not need a surfboard now, all she needed was a wave! The excitement of the ride was all that Mimi now did crave!

She waited as the sun shone down for the big wave to arrive; she watched around as all the fish and sharks and whales would dive!

The wave was right behind her now and Mimi waited on, it picked her up and she rode fast until the wave was gone.

Kids Books By Naila

Coming soon! More Stories to engage your adventurous spirit!

Available on Amazon now!!

Available on paperback now at www.kidsbooksbynaila.com and www.kidsbooksbynaila.ca

More Stories To Come

- Sammy Spiders Rock Wall
- Polly's Mom
- Ali's Journey
- Archie's True Wish
- The Rooster Alarm
- Eileen's Home

www.ingramcontent.com/pod-product-compliance
Lightning Source LLC
Chambersburg PA
CBHW042128040426
42450CB00002B/115